# The Positive Affirmations Handbook

## How to Create and Use Affirmations That Work

Nathalie Thompson

For information visit the author's web sites at:

www.NathalieThompson.com
www.VibeShifting.com.

ISBN: 978-0-9948844-4-2 (ebk)
ISBN: 978-0-9948844-7-3 (pbk)

# Table of Contents

# Introduction

CHANGE YOUR THOUGHTS AND YOU
CHANGE YOUR WORLD.
~NORMAN VINCENT PEALE

What would it mean to you if you could finally start making progress towards your biggest dreams? What would it be like if you finally *believed* in yourself and in your own ability to achieve the goals that matter most to you? What would you give if you could stop worrying all the time and finally start moving forward with your life, despite your fears?

I'm guessing that having that kind of self-confidence and success would mean the world to you. But how many times have you already tried and failed to achieve something important? How many times have you poured all your energy and best intentions into something, and still had nothing to show for all that effort? What happened then?

Perhaps you found yourself "just"-ifying your experience by saying things like:

- "It's just too hard."
- "I'm just not good enough to get there."
- "I guess I'm just not meant to succeed."

If you have ever tried to make a change in your life, only to find yourself disappointed with the results, you know how painful and frustrating it can be. You know how much of a toll it can take on your self-confidence and self-esteem, and how much it can scare you off the thought of ever trying to reach that goal again.

When we fail at something in which we are emotionally invested, our tendency is to make ourselves feel even smaller by focusing on all the personal characteristics or perceived personal flaws that *we believe* precipitated our inevitable failure. The inner critic inside of us comes charging to the front of our minds, telling us how useless we are and confirming our worst fears that we will never, ever, be enough to achieve or become what we most want to.

But here's the secret about all of that: despite what your inner critic is telling you, it's not you. You're not the problem. More than that, you've never been the problem. As I mention in my book *Mind Shifting*, the biggest reason most people fail to achieve their goals is not because they're doing something wrong, it's because there's something wrong with their subconscious *thoughts*.

> Your failures are a result of a problem
> with your subconscious thought processes;
> they are not a comment on YOU as a person.

Lack of success is a symptom of a problem with your mindset and mental programming. It is not a comment on your worthiness as a person. But changing that underlying, faulty mental programming is obviously critical if you want to start achieving and experiencing what you really want in life.

It's so simple in theory, but sometimes it's much harder to do in practice because one of the biggest things we all have to deal with when trying to make any kind of lasting changes in our lives is the constant barrage of negative and self-defeating thoughts that we subject ourselves to on a daily basis. We all tend to be much harder on ourselves than we are on anybody else, and that can have a very detrimental effect on our ability to follow through with our goals.

# Hacking Your Subconscious

One of the best tools I've found for making permanent changes to my own faulty programming is the use of affirmations. They're the best way to hack that buggy mental software so that you can fix it. Affirmations can help you in two main ways:

1. They can help you become more self-empowered.

2. They can help you to finally make the changes you want to see in your life.

Essentially, affirmations help you to reprogram your subconscious mind. They work by putting an end to all the automated negative thinking that you've put in place over the course of your life and replacing it with more useful thought patterns.

In turn, replacing negative patterns with positive patterns will help you to become more confident and more likely to achieve your goals because you'll be less likely to fall into the pessimist's trap of accepting bad situations as they are without even trying to do anything about them.

Pessimists like to complain about things. Optimists choose to find solutions to their problems and create a better reality.

In other words, pessimists like to complain about things but they never bother trying to change the things they don't like because they truly believe that things cannot be changed. Optimists, however, can see alternatives. They believe in their own ability to change things for the better. They look for solutions to their problems, and then they go out and implement them.

## Making the Shift

This is the threefold gift that a positive mindset will bring you:

1. The ability to see the potential for a different reality;

2. The strength to seek out as many different paths and solutions as needed to get yourself there; and

3. The determination and resilience to follow those new paths and make it happen.

Affirmations are one of the most effective tools at your disposal for making this kind of mindset shift.

The whole point of using affirmations is to permanently change your ingrained thoughts and belief system with regards to whatever it is you are trying to achieve. If you ever want to *live* the life you dream about, you need to believe in yourself and your own ability to create that new reality.

If there is something that you really want, but at the same time you don't really believe that it's possible, you will not achieve it because you will subconsciously sabotage your own efforts to get there. You cannot make a change in your life if you don't believe you are capable of it or that you deserve it, so the most important thing you need to do is change your belief system with regards to the those life changes or goals that you want.

Learning how to create affirmations will help you do this because changing your thoughts really *can* change your world!

## What This Book Will Do For You

Figuring out how to silence your own inner critic can be a challenging task, but it's a critical step if you want to see real change happening in your life.

And that's what *The Positive Affirmations Handbook* is all about – helping you to silence your nasty gremlins so that you can get back to the business of living the kind of life *you* want, without being dragged down by all those scary voices in your own head that insist on telling you that you can't, that you're not good enough, and that you'll never get to where you want to be.

There is something inside of you that knows those voices are wrong, but you've been listening to them for so long now that you've forgotten how to fight back and make your own decisions, in your own best interests. You've forgotten how to be the person you always wanted to be – the kind of person you were always *meant* to be.

> You've forgotten how to be the person you always wanted to be – the kind of person you were always *meant* to be.

This book will help you with all of that. You will learn:

- What affirmations are (and what they aren't);
- How to spot and avoid positive thinking pitfalls before they derail you;
- How to create your own personalized affirmations – that actually work;
- What to do when you run into problems and your affirmations aren't producing results; and,
- How to power up your affirmations with advanced mindset techniques.

By the time you've finished *The Positive Affirmations Handbook*, you're going to be an affirmations expert, with all the power you need to battle your inner critics and start living your life on your own terms.

# Chapter 1:
# What are Affirmations?

IF YOU REALIZED JUST HOW POWERFUL
YOUR THOUGHTS ARE, YOU WOULD NEVER
THINK A NEGATIVE THOUGHT.
~PEACE PILGRIM

To begin using affirmations effectively, you must first understand what they are and what they are used for. And our definition is really very simple: Affirmations are a set of positive statements that you repeat to yourself in order to change your ingrained ways of thinking and shift yourself from automatic negative thoughts to automatic positive thoughts.

Affirmations can be used to help you with just about anything you want to achieve or manifest in your life. The key is to figure out what's at the heart of whatever it is that you want, and then use affirmations that will help you in those key areas. So, if you're trying to become more optimistic, you might use the affirmation "I look for the positive in every situation". If you're looking to become more successful in business, you could use "I am successful in everything I do."

The point is to change the way you *feel* about whatever it is you are trying to achieve, because it is not just our thoughts that shape our experiences, it is the *feelings* associated with those thoughts. By shifting the way we feel, we shift the energy we are sending out into the Universe, and we *change the future itself* because what we give out is what comes back to us, every time.

By shifting the way we feel, we are shifting the energy we send out into the Universe and changing the future itself.

The late Wayne Dyer once said: "Loving people live in a loving world. Hostile people live in a hostile world. Same world." In other words, you experience the kind of world you *expect* to experience. And those expectations are created within your own mind, within your own beliefs and your own emotions. You *must* change what's happening on the inside before you can ever experience a change on the outside.

# What Affirmations Don't Do

For all their power, it's also important to understand that there are a lot of things that affirmations can't and won't do for you:

- They are not a miracle cure for depression or any other illness.
- They don't work instantly.
- They can't make you believe something you're not ready to believe.

That last point is key, and it's one of the biggest stumbling blocks that people run into when trying to use positive affirmations to effect personal change.

> Affirmations cannot make you believe something you're not ready to believe.

This is really important because if you use them wrongly, affirmations can sometimes backfire on you and make things worse than they were before. (But don't worry – we'll go over the right way to use them, and what to do when you're not getting any results later in the book!)

# Affirmations vs Mantras

Before we move on, there is one more thing that we should clear up: Another concept that you've likely heard of in your personal development journey is that of a "mantra". Sometimes people use this word interchangeably with "affirmation", but they're not really the same thing.

### Mantras and affirmations are not the same things.

When most people think of a mantra it's usually in association with meditation. And in that sense, the word probably conjures up pictures in your mind of people sitting around with their eyes closed, chanting "om". When I talk about mantras, however, it's more in the sense of a personal catchphrase or motto; something that you can use as a compass point in your life.

More specifically, and for the purposes of this book, I use the term "mantra" to mean a single word, or sometimes a phrase, that provides you with an immediate boost of focus, confidence, or creativity. And I use the term "affirmation" to mean a positive sentence or phrase used to alter an underlying, problematic mental program.

# Quick-Fix or Lasting Change?

The Merriam-Webster online dictionary defines a mantra as "a mystical formula of invocation or incantation"[1], a definition I love, because it makes me think of all things magical. And to me, mantras really are something magical.

It's like having your own personal spell that you can whisper to yourself when times get tough. Something to remind you of your goals and everything — all the hopes and dreams and work you've already put in — that lies behind those goals. And it gives you the strength to keep going. A mantra instantly re-inspires and reinvigorates you, like magic. But that boost is temporary.

> Mantras work fast but don't last.
> Affirmations take time and effort but the results can last a lifetime.

Mantras are like cold-and-flu medications that allow you to keep working despite your misery, but they don't fix the underlying problem. They can mask symptoms but they don't provide a *cure* for what's *causing* those symptoms. So when the "magic" wears off, you're right back where you started.

To put it another way: mantras work fast but don't last. Affirmations take time and effort but, when used properly, the results can last a lifetime.

# Chapter 2:
# When NOT to Use
# Affirmations

AFFIRMATIONS DON'T MAKE SOMETHING HAPPEN;
THEY MAKE SOMETHING WELCOME.
~MICHAEL BERNARD BECKWITH

Are affirmations ever a bad thing? Can they be dangerous or even make our situations worse than they already are? The short answer: Yes. The long answer: Only if you don't understand how they work and end up using them the wrong way.

Obviously, you want to know how to use them the *right* way so that you don't run into this problem and end up with all your hard work backfiring on you.

There's nothing worse than doing something to try and help yourself and then having things go even further south because of your efforts!

Now, when we talk about the downsides to affirmations, we have to look at them within the broader context of positive thinking in general, and how that kind of mindset can sometimes have unintended consequences. And, believe it or not, there *are* peer-reviewed scientific studies out there that show significant downsides to positive thinking.

## The Downside of Positive Thinking

A 2009 study published in *Psychological Science*[2] by researchers at the University of Waterloo in Canada found that, while people with high self-esteem benefited from the use of positive self-statements (affirmations) people with low self-esteem who used affirmations ended up feeling worse than they did before.

On the surface, this might be seen as making positive thinking and specifically affirmations look bad (and there are more than a few people out there referencing this particular study as "proof" that positive thinking is a bad thing). But from a Law of Attraction perspective, the outcome of this study actually makes perfect sense.

Law of Attraction (LOA) tells us that what we send out into the world is what comes back to us ("as within, so without"). From this, we understand that what we are focused on, and in alignment with, is what we manifest into our lives. So the automatic assumption for many people is that focusing on the positive and squashing all forms of negativity is the only way to go.

A lot of LOA types push the positive thinking thing for precisely this reason. But the problem is that trying to squash out negativity doesn't work. When you resist something this way, you're actually focusing on it. And trying to force positivity when you're really not there is not only ineffective, it can actually be harmful. Sometimes, dealing with the negative is not only appropriate, it's necessary. Likewise, there are times when optimism is not only foolish, it's dangerous.

## Positivity Pitfalls to Avoid

Some of the more problematic elements of misused positive thinking include: delusional thinking; complacency and inaction; repression/denial of feelings; and blaming the victims. In fact, these are the five most common positivity pitfalls that you'll want to avoid when working with your affirmations.

Let's take a closer look at each of them so that you can recognize and steer yourself around them...

## Delusional Thinking.

This stems from the mistaken belief that any kind of negative thinking is a disaster waiting to happen and it leads to a pig-headed and extremely dangerous refusal to even contemplate any potential negative consequences of one's actions.

If your metaphorical car is racing headlong towards a cliff, for instance, sitting there affirming that "it's all good and everything will work out fine" is not only delusional, it's suicidal; step on the damn brakes and stop the car!

## Complacency and Inaction.

Another valid criticism of positive thinking is that it can lead to complacency – getting stuck in the happy-thoughts mode, but never actually *doing* anything with your life.

If you want to manifest awesome things and experiences for yourself, *you* have to go out and make them happen. Thinking positive thoughts and fantasizing about possibilities is a great tool for inspiring yourself to action, as long as you actually get to the *action* part of things. Spending your entire life daydreaming about what *could be* is a waste of your life. Get out there, do something and BE awesome instead of just thinking about it.

## Repression/Denial of Feelings.

Oftentimes, when faced with the view that one should always look on the bright side of things, people mistakenly believe that they should stamp out any negative emotions they may have. Not only is this dangerous, it never works.

Our emotions are there for a reason, and trying to suppress an emotion because we think it's "bad" only causes harm. There *are* no bad emotions. All of our emotions are there to give us feedback about where our energy and focus is directed.

> There *are* no bad emotions. All of our emotions are there to give us feedback about where our energy and focus is directed.

If you're feeling sad, or angry, or jealous, this is important information to know. And emotions take time to process. Sometimes, you just have to let them run their course before you can move up the emotional scale to a better feeling place. Trying to squash a feeling before you've dealt with it just keeps you trapped there, preventing you from ever being able to move on.

Also, there is something to be said for the idea that we need the duality of positive and negative in order to appreciate the good in life. If there was no darkness, we would never be able to see the stars. Likewise, without the negative, we might never come to know the strength that we have or appreciate the blessings that are already around us without taking them for granted.

## Blaming the Victims.

Positive thinking is also sometimes used to support a "blame the victim" mentality. This can, unfortunately, lead people who are suffering from things like cancer, or people who experience trauma in their lives, to blame themselves for their situations.

It's especially troubling when positivity is used as an excuse for callousness or lack of compassion for others who are suffering, because they are viewed as having "brought it on themselves". People who are new to Law of Attraction and don't fully understand it yet, for instance, are often particularly susceptible to this kind of mindset.

Positive thinking should *never* be used as an excuse for cruel disregard for human suffering of any sort.

Blaming the victims is probably one of the most insidious, harmful, and distressing dangers of misused positive thinking. And it's NOT what positivity is or should be about.

If you're in such situation, *it's not your fault* and this did *not* happen to you because you weren't positive enough. This cannot be stressed enough. Yes, there are vibrational and energy issues at play, but these things tend to be complicated, with many variables at play, and they are never conscious.

Positive thinking should *never* be used as an excuse for cruel disregard for human suffering of any sort.

# Why Think Positive At All?

So, after all these positivity pitfalls, you may be thinking that the dangerous aspects of positive thinking outweigh the good. But it still has far more pluses than minuses. One of the biggest benefits of positive thinking is that it allows us to *hope*.

When everything is bleak, looking for the positive in our situation keeps us from falling into that bottomless pit of despair and hopelessness; it gives us the ability to believe in something better and galvanizes us to *do* something to *make* the situation better.

One of the biggest benefits of positive thinking is that it allows us to *hope*.

At the very least, looking for the positive allows us to live our lives with an element of peace that we might not otherwise experience. And perhaps it might even provide us with some amount of joy, which is something that every one of us needs and deserves.

Affirmations are just one way of harnessing the power of positivity to change our thought habits so that we may change our experience of life. And with that in mind, in the next chapter we're going to learn how to create them the *right* way.

# Chapter 3:
# How to Create Affirmations

THE GREATEST DISCOVERY OF ALL TIME IS THAT
A PERSON CAN CHANGE HIS FUTURE MERELY
BY CHANGING HIS ATTITUDE.
~OPRAH WINFREY

By this point, you've likely realized that affirmations are one of the most powerful vibe-shifting tools we have at our disposal. But you're probably wondering how to create affirmations that will help you achieve that kind of shift. How do you know what affirmations to use, and how can you make sure they'll actually work?

Don't panic – it's not as hard or as scary as it might sound. In fact, you can create effective personalized affirmations with just five simple steps:

1. Figure out what you want.
2. Turn it into a statement.
3. Be positive.
4. Be realistic.
5. Repeat, repeat, repeat!

That's really all there is to it. But let's break those steps down a bit more and see how they work...

# The Five-Step Process

## Step 1: Figure out what you want.

What is it that you are trying to create or manifest in your life? What is the end result you're aiming for, and what behaviours or attitudes will you need to get yourself there?

For example, do you want to live a healthier lifestyle? Do you want to handle stress better? Meet the love of your life? Have more friends? Be more successful in your business or at school? What is it that *you* want for yourself?

And in order to achieve these things, what will you need to do or become? For example, will you need to learn how to relax more? Will you need to become more outgoing or overcome your shyness? Ask yourself what personal attributes you will need to cultivate in order to achieve your goal.

### Step 2: Turn it into a statement.

Once you're clear on what you want, you need to turn it into a few short statements or sentences that define that vision for you. Try to put these phrases in present tense wherever possible, and don't use "want" statements. In other words, "I am relaxed and peaceful" is better than "I want to be more relaxed".

The reason for putting the phrase in the present tense is that you're trying to make your subconscious mind believe that it's already a foregone conclusion. You're trying to manifest having/achieving the thing, rather than manifesting more "wanting" of the thing.

Focus on *having* whatever it is that you want, rather than on *wanting* whatever it is that you don't yet have.

This is a critical distinction. Focusing on wanting something only brings you more wanting of the thing, because if you "want" you don't actually "have" yet. Our thoughts and feelings create our experiences and shape our world, so focus on what it would *feel* like to already be living what you want, rather than focusing on the thing you want itself.

## Step 3: Be positive.

When you're creating your statements, you want to make sure they are positive. You're trying to program your subconscious to believe these statements, so you want to focus completely on what you want rather than on what you *don't* want. For example, use "I am relaxed and peaceful" rather than "I am less stressed."

The problem with the second statement is that your subconscious mind tends to filter out concepts like "not", and focuses instead on the "stress". And again, what you're focused on is what you end up creating for yourself. If you want to rid yourself of stress then stop thinking about *avoiding* stress and start thinking about *promoting* relaxation and tranquility instead.

## Step 4: Be realistic.

Sometimes, especially if you're new to using affirmations, making a statement that is too far beyond your current experience will just cause your inner critic to jump in and shut you down before you even get started.

## The key is to create a positive statement that still feels realistic to you.

For example, "I am always peaceful and relaxed" may be too big of a jump for your current situation. If you've been feeling very stressed out and frazzled, and try to use that particular affirmation right off the bat, your mind might automatically call "bullshit" and make it impossible for you to believe it.

If that's the case, then try something like "I become more relaxed every day" or "I am learning to relax more and more". The key is to create a positive statement that helps you make progress towards your goal without triggering any objections from that negative little voice inside.

This is about incremental improvement rather than quantum leaps. That doesn't mean that it has to take a long time to get what you want, but it does mean that there is a process to your affirmations. It's like that old adage: the only way to eat an elephant is to do it one bite at a time.

Aim for incremental changes over time rather than sudden quantum leaps that might trigger your inner critic.

To put it another way: you'll achieve more by telling yourself that you can pick up one small stone today – and then *doing* it, every day – than you will by telling yourself you can move a mountain and immediately getting overwhelmed by the enormity of it all and giving up in despair before you've even gotten started.

Create affirmations that help you make little changes that will add up over time rather than trying for enormous changes that will immediately trigger your inner critic and sabotage any further efforts to make *any* change at all.

### Step 5: Repeat, repeat, repeat!

Repetition is the key to making your affirmations work for you because you're trying to change your beliefs about what is possible for you and your own reality. A belief is just a thought that you have formed a habit of thinking, so if you change that habit and start deliberately thinking new thoughts, you will change your belief. Using your affirmations frequently will help to make them your new habit.

And that's all there is to it! Just five simple steps to create effective, personal affirmations that will help you achieve any goal.

You can use this five-step strategy as often as you like to help you achieve any dream or goal that you have. It doesn't matter whether the dream is big or small, or whether the goal is creative or business oriented – the process is always going to be the same.

# Chapter 4:
# How to Use Affirmations

A BELIEF IS JUST A THOUGHT
YOU KEEP THINKING.
~ESTHER HICKS

Now you know what affirmations are good for, what to beware of when using them, and how to make your own, personalized, affirmations. So the question now becomes: *how* do you use them?

Do affirmations work best when they are written or spoken? How often should they be used in a day? Are there any specific rules about how to use affirmations to make energy shifts and align yourself with what you want in life? We're going to answer all of these questions in the next few sections.

# When to Use Affirmations

The best time of day to use your affirmations depends completely upon you and your own lifestyle and habits. You can use your affirmations:

- As a tool to help you relax before you go to sleep at night.
- First thing in the morning to help you program your day.
- During the day to remind yourself of what you're trying to manifest.

You can use affirmations anywhere and everywhere, as often as you feel is right for you. I like to use them at night, just before bed, because I like the idea of my subconscious mind mulling over my new positive thoughts all night long while I'm asleep. I also sometimes use them first thing in the morning, to help set the tone for the day.

Aside from morning and evening, you can even use affirmations throughout the day. Try repeating them to yourself, either silently or out loud, whenever you want to remind yourself of all the awesomeness you're working to create for yourself. It's a great way to spend idle time when you're commuting to and from work, or standing in line at photocopiers or coffee shops!

# Spoken vs Written Affirmations

One of the questions that I am frequently asked about affirmations is whether they work best when you say them out loud or when you write them down and then read them. This depends mostly on what *feels* right for you, but if you're not sure where to start, I usually recommend a mix of both.

### The Case for Written Affirmations

I like using written affirmations because you can put them on little sticky notes and then leave them in strategic places where you are likely to see them frequently throughout your day. For example, you can put them inside cupboards, at the edge of your computer screen, tucked inside your lunch bag, etc. Each time you happen upon one of your stealthily planted affirmation notes, it provides a little energy boost and helps to reinforce the "new program" that you are trying to "code" into your mind.

> Written affirmations are powerful because your brain is hardwired to read text instantly.

Written affirmations are powerful because the human brain (once trained to read, obviously) is wired to instantly and automatically read any written words it encounters. Frequently seeing your affirmations in print, therefore, will definitely help you absorb those thoughts and feelings faster.

(Side note: For a quick demonstration of how the brain's automatic word-reading ability works, be sure to check out the psychological phenomenon known as the "Stroop Effect"[3] and see for yourself how powerful the written word is!)

## The Case for Spoken Affirmations

While I am huge fan of written, leave-'em-everywhere affirmations, I do recommend that people also use spoken affirmations. Why? For a couple of reasons, actually:

1. The voice with the most powerful influence on you is always your own, so speaking your affirmations aloud is a great way to super-charge them.

2. When you speak your affirmations aloud, you get instant body feedback on what you're really feeling about them.

That second point is important: if you're not really in alignment with what you're trying to manifest via your affirmations, you will instantly be aware of it through a tightening in your chest, or an uneasy feeling in your stomach, for example.

Everyone's physical reactions are different, so what you feel may be different than what someone else would feel, but if you're paying attention you'll always get some sort of body feedback when you speak your affirmations.

This means that simply talking out loud and saying your affirmations will give you valuable information about where your alignment currently stands with respect to your "new program".

> If you're paying attention you'll always get some sort of biofeedback when you speak your affirmations.

If you feel great when you're saying your affirmations, then keep going and have fun! If you're not feeling so good when you say them, you know that you still have work to do in order to make your vibrational shift (in which case, see Chapter 6 for alignment exercises that can help you to power up your affirmations).

## How Often Should You Use Affirmations?

When it comes to affirmations, the more often you can fit them into your day, the better! This is why using a mix of written and spoken affirmations can really help to make this tool work for you.

Also, don't be afraid to get creative! If you want to sing your affirmations in the shower, or paint them across a canvas, or write them in the sand on the beach, go for it! There are no hard-and-fast rules about how to use affirmations to help you manifest your dreams and goals. The best way to use them is in a way that feels right *to you* and helps to generate excitement, joy, and positive feelings about what you want to create or achieve.

# Chapter 5:
# When Affirmations Don't Work

MOST OF US HAVE TWO LIVES.
THE LIFE WE LIVE, AND THE UNLIVED LIFE WITHIN US.
BETWEEN THE TWO STANDS RESISTANCE.
~STEVEN PRESSFIELD

In Chapter 3 you learned the five-step process for creating affirmations that work, and you learned that step four was to ensure that your affirmations are realistic. This is the critical point that was missed in the Waterloo study that you learned about in Chapter 2 that found affirmations could be harmful in people with low self-esteem.

The single confounding factor at the heart of every failed affirmation is simply this: **you didn't really believe it**. If you don't believe your affirmations, they won't work, and can even make things worse.

I once got an email from a blog reader who wanted to know how she could "control her mind" in order to live a happier life. She had dealt with a lot of bad situations in her life, and was struggling to cope with other people's negativity. She wanted so much to believe that she could change her outlook by changing her thoughts, but she also felt that her mind was rejecting all her attempts to use affirmations and visualize happy days as being "fake".

The more emotionally attached you are
to the outcome you want, the harder
it can seem to make it happen.

So here's what's happening in this kind of situation: When you're having problems trying to make changes in life or trying to manifest something important to you, the setbacks you encounter along your journey can sometimes seem insurmountable. And the more emotionally attached you are to the outcome you want, the harder it can seem to make it happen. This is especially true when the changes you want to make are very different from what you are currently experiencing.

It's not that the changes you want are hard, in and of themselves. What's happening here is, again, that problem with *belief* — you have to believe your affirmations before they can work for you. And if your affirmation statements are so far beyond your current reality that they seem unfathomable, then you won't believe them, no matter how often you desperately repeat them in an effort to brainwash yourself into positivity. It just doesn't work that way.

An affirmation statement that you don't believe deep down in your core *will* backfire on you. Not only will it fail to help you manifest what you want, it may actually cause harm by making you give up on what you want because it now feels even further away than before.

Affirmations must be positive, and they must take you in the direction you want to go, but they must still be *believable* if they are to be effective.

This is not blaming you for failing to "do affirmations right". You didn't know this key piece of information before, so how could you possibly be expected to make things work without it? It's like getting that cool new toy for your birthday when you were a kid - the one that looked so amazing in all the advertisements - and then tearing open the box in anticipation, only to find that there was "some assembly required" and "batteries not included". You can't expect your affirmations to work properly when you're missing a critical component.

## Wanting a Change is the First Step

If you're in the same situation as my blog reader, wherein you really want this "affirmations stuff" to work but struggle with nagging doubts that it's all fake, hokey, woo-woo, hippie-dippy, New-Age crap... fear not. Woo-woo though it may look on the outside, most of this LOA stuff can be explained with "real" human psychology. It's just a different way of talking about it, that's all.

Also, the first step in making any change in life is the realization that you have a *desire* to make that change. The fact that you want to change your mindset and make a shift from a negative outlook to a more positive outlook is wonderful, and it means that things could start changing for you fairly quickly. So don't lose hope, even though it seems like you're not making any progress so far.

The first step in making any change in life
is the realization that you have a *desire*
to make that change.

The cause of your current frustration, and what you're most likely dealing with right now is what we call "resistance", and if you're interested in learning more about the topic of resistance, there is an entire chapter devoted to it in my book, *fearLESS*. For the purposes of this book, however, what you need to know about resistance is simply this: When you're having a problem with affirmations, what's usually happening is that you're trying to make too big of a mental and emotional stretch too soon. You can't jump from a really negative mindset to a really positive one all at once – it's just too different from what you've gotten used to. Your subconscious mind is feeling threatened by this experience gap and, because of that, it is interfering in your ability to create the change you want.

## When Resistance Strikes, Start Small

So, what we do when we're experiencing this kind of resistance? We start smaller. Much smaller. Dial down your affirmations so that they're less likely to set off any subconscious alarms.

If, like our blog reader, you're in a difficult situation and everything seems hopelessly bleak, then instead of waking up and telling yourself "This is going to be a happy day", which just makes your subconscious mind yell "Yeah right! It's not going to be a happy day, it's never a happy day!" you start with something less threatening. Try something like "Maybe today will be a little bit better than yesterday. I'm open to things being just a tiny bit better than they were yesterday. After all, stranger things have happened. Days that are a little bit less bad *could* happen."

Reaching for something that is just a little bit better, that *feels* just a little bit better, than where you are now will help to move you closer to where you want to be without waking that cranky dragon in your mind. If you can keep from rousing the dragon's suspicions that you're trying to change the situation that it has become used to, it won't try to interfere so much. Use a stealth attack and fly below the resistance radar with your affirmation statements, or you're just going to get shot down.

## What Gratitude Does

The other thing that I would absolutely recommend, and thing that will probably make the biggest difference in your life, is that every night before you go to sleep, think back through your day and deliberately look for good things that happened.

Genuine gratitude for what we already have in life is one of the most powerful tools we have available to us.

Look for three good things that happened *every single day*, and don't stop looking until you find those three things (at *least* three). Even if all you can think of are things like "it was sunny" or "the girl at the coffee shop said hello to me" or "I got a parking space that was closer to the building than usual". Find three things that were good and concentrate on feeling a sense of joyful appreciation for them.

Genuine gratitude for what we already have in life, even when we have very little, is one of the most powerful tools we have available to us. Do this exercise every night before you go to sleep, and it *will* start to make a big difference in your life.

Focusing on what is already good
in your life helps to pave the way for
even more positive things to manifest
themselves into your reality.

By focusing on anything that is already good and happy, you will start to make a mental and vibrational shift that will help to pave the way for even more positive things to manifest into your life.

## Why is it Taking So Long?

Another interesting question I once received from a different blog reader asked why it was taking so long to manifest a particular desire into her life. This is a sentiment that a lot of frustrated affirmations-users can sympathize with. When our affirmations aren't paying off with tangible results in the time frames we were hoping for, it can often make us wonder whether they're even working at all.

## Impatience is a sign that you're focused on lack.

Here's the Catch-22 in this: impatience is a sign of an alignment issue. Remember what you learned in Chapter 3 about aligning yourself with what you want rather than what you don't want? When you're frustrated by a lack of progress and feeling impatient, what do you think you are aligned with? You're aligned with the feeling that what you want isn't here yet. You're focused on the *lack* of the thing or experience, so that is what you continue to manifest: more lack and more frustration.

The only way to get yourself out of this mind trap is to stop spinning the wheel you're on. Take a moment to let yourself feel what you feel: anger, frustration, despair... whatever it is, just *feel* it. But do it consciously. Rather than getting swept up in your feelings, let them sweep *over* you and then away from you. Think of your emotions like a river – they are always flowing through you, and they are always changing. If you remain still and try to just observe them instead of getting caught up in them, they will follow the current and flow on by. Acknowledge them but don't get stuck in them.

## How to Flip Your Fears

In other words, if, as you observe what you're feeling you realize that you are frustrated and afraid that things will never change, say that out loud or write it down. For example: "I am frustrated! This is taking so long and I'm so scared that I'm going to run out of time or money before I can make it happen!"

If additional thoughts and fears come bubbling to the surface as you do this exercise, then keep writing. All the thoughts, all the fears, all the feelings... write it all out. But don't stop there. Remember what I said about not getting stuck in bad feelings? Now that you know what you're dealing with, go through what you've written and pull all the main themes out into a bullet-point list. These are the big issues that are keeping you stuck – they're the thoughts and beliefs that are preventing your affirmations from working for you.

Once you have your list, flip each of these points around. What would your ideal counter-point to each of them be? For example, if one of your bullet points is that you hate your job but you're terrified of losing it, then the counter point might be that you wish you could find a job that you love and that you're good at and where you feel safe and appreciated.

Once you've made all your counter points, turn each one into a new affirmation (and remember not to push it so far that it stretches you beyond your ability to believe). For example: "I am willing to consider that the perfect job might be out there for me." Or: "I believe that the perfect job is out there waiting for me right now." Or even: "Someone out there is looking to hire someone just like me!"

# Chapter 6:
# Powering Up Your Affirmations

ONCE YOU REPLACE NEGATIVE THOUGHTS
WITH POSITIVE ONES, YOU'LL START
HAVING POSITIVE RESULTS.
~WILLIE NELSON

So now you have all of the basic knowledge and tools that you need to create your own affirmations and start making big changes in your life. But what I want to do now is give you three advanced strategies that you can use in conjunction with your affirmations. These strategies will help you to power up your manifesting mojo and really start working miracles in your life!

These strategies are: energy ladders, achievement boards, and evidence journals. They will help you to make even bigger shifts in your thoughts and feelings about what you want, and will keep you focused on creating those changes for yourself.

# Energy Ladders

The fastest way to ramp up your affirmations is to get your alignment in order. Remember that the number one reason affirmations fail is because you tried to use a statement that was so far beyond your current reality that you couldn't bring yourself to believe it.

Remember also that that all energy work is about emotion rather than intellect. No matter how well you understand the principles behind a practice, you have to *feel* it before you can use it effectively.

Energy work is about shifting your emotions and beliefs so that you are able to *allow* what you want to manifest into your life.

An energy ladder is a simple but powerful means of helping you with those all-important feelings. It's a means of getting your mindset and emotions focused on and aligned with what it is that you really want so that you can *allow* it to manifest into your life.

Remember that it's not what you *say* you want or what you *think* you want that is the determining factor in what you manifest into your reality. When we want something in life, it is never about the thing itself, it's about what lies behind the thing. It's about how we think having the thing will make us *feel*. And those feelings are based on the *meaning* that we attribute to those things.

When we want something in life, it is never about the thing itself, it's about how we think having the thing will make us *feel*.

The ladder is a quick and easy way of clarifying those underlying emotions and meanings so that you are consciously aware of what is truly important about what you're trying to create. It helps you to really understand the *what* and the *why* of things, without getting tangled up in the messy *how* (which isn't your business anyway – leave that part up to the Universe!)

### How to Create Your Ladder

So how does it work? My suggestion is that you find a nice quiet place where you can sit or lie down comfortably and not be interrupted for a few minutes. Focus on what you're trying manifest. As an example, let's say you want a new, awesome relationship in your life – you're trying to manifest "The One". So focus on that. And think about what having that relationship in your life would feel like.

Do *not* start focusing on a specific individual! Focus solely on the feelings surrounding the relationship itself. And then just let it build like the rungs of a ladder – let one feeling lead to another and focus on each one as it floats to the surface of your mind.

For example, an energy ladder focused on manifesting Mr. or Ms. Right into your life might involve cascading statements such as:

- It feels easy; like it's supposed to happen.
- It feels natural; like it's meant to be.
- It feels safe. It feels like safety.
- It feels like sunshine. Like Light itself.
- It feels playful. It feels open. It feels like trust.
- It feels passionate! It feels exciting!
- It feels fun! It feels joyful and free!
- It feels like exhilaration! It feels like bubbling laughter!
- It feels like home. It feels like belonging.
- It feels like hope. It feels like love.

For some, it helps to imagine a grid or a network, rather than a ladder, and as each feeling comes to mind it fills in a grid square or lights up a network node rather than adding a ladder rung. But if that doesn't work for you, you don't even need to get that detailed. What's important about energy ladders is to focus on the *feelings* that lie at the heart of what you want and to just let one lead to the next. Let those feelings flow for about a minute and a half – that's all it takes to shift your energy and your alignment, which in turn makes your affirmations more powerful.

# Achievement Boards

The second power-up strategy that you can use is an achievement board. An achievement board is a specific type of vision board, and a vision board is a powerful tool for helping you to focus on your goals and dreams. These boards can provide encouragement and motivation to help you see your goals through to completion. On top of that, they're just plain fun to put together!

An achievement board will motivate and energize you to achieve your goals.

An achievement board is a collection of images, words and phrases whose meanings evoke the *nature* or *personal meaning* of your specific goals (the things you want to achieve or manifest). A board can be tangible, like an actual piece of poster board or a journal that you glue and write your images and things onto, or it can be electronic, like a folder on your computer's hard drive where you store all your images and phrases, or a collage you put together in a graphics program like Photoshop, Canva, or even a word processing program like Microsoft Word.

You can even make digital achievement boards online using Pinterest[4], where you have the option of making your board public (to increase your accountability to get things done) or secret (if you're not yet ready to share your dreams with the world and would prefer to keep them private).

You can have one big vision board with everything on it all at once, or you can have separate vision boards dedicated to specific things or experiences that you want to manifest, or particular areas of your life that you want to change.

For best results, choose material for your achievement board that holds real emotional impact (in a good way)!

The most important thing to understand when creating an achievement board is that all of the images and phrases in your board should have some real emotions tied to them that inspire you, excite you, and motivate you to do what you've set out to do. You want to feel awesome when you look at this board, so choose your images and phrases wisely, and feel free to update, add, and delete as your goals evolve.

## How to Create an Achievement Board

Whether you choose to create a hard-copy or digital achievement board, here's a simple method for creating a board that will motivate and energize you to follow through with your goals...

### Step 1: Set Your Goals.

Write down one of the goals you want to achieve this year. For example:

- "I want to lose ten pounds."
- "I want to make an extra $10 000"
- "I want to release my own album"

### Step 2: Clarify Your "Why".

Write down *why* you want to achieve this goal. Remember to keep your language positive when you do this — thinking about these goals should make you feel good! For example:

- "Because I'll feel healthy and sexy." (**NOT** "Because I feel fat")
- "Because it will make me feel secure." (**NOT** "Because I never have enough")
- "Because it would be so much fun." (**NOT** "Because I never took my music seriously enough")

### Step 3: Choose Your Key Words.

What one word embodies the quality or internal state that you think achieving this goal will bring you? Use your reason statement from step 2 for clues. For example:

- "sexy", "healthy", "confident"
- "security", "freedom", "safe"
- "fun", "excitement", "create"

### Step 4: Define Your Action Steps.

What physical action will you take to make this goal a reality? Pick a word or a phrase, or find an image, that symbolizes this action. For example:

- "yoga", "walk", "eat healthy"
- "invest", "launch my own business"
- "find a writing partner", "sing"

### Step 5: Inspire Yourself.

Finally, pick an inspirational quote or create a mantra that motivates you to accomplish your goals this year. Make it something that really clicks or resonates with you and ties all the above steps together.

Once you've completed all five steps, put all of the images, words, quotes and phrases you've pulled together into your achievement board. When you're done with one goal, you can go then go through the above method for each of the goals you've set for yourself this year, either creating a new board for each goal, or putting all your goals together in one big achievement board.

### For An Extra Kick...

You'll want to refer to your achievement board often to keep yourself grounded and motivated to keep moving forward, so be sure to make it as appealing as you can. And you don't need to limit yourself to words, quotes, and images when finding material for inspiration! If you've decided to go digital, the sky is pretty much the limit for what you can add, and you may choose to include things like:

- song lyrics;
- MP3 files;
- links to inspirational YouTube videos; or
- links to helpful blog articles.

Whatever bits and pieces you find that make you feel jazzed about your goal, that make you feel awesome and happy, enthusiastic and energized – anything that makes you feel *good* about your goal is perfect fodder for your achievement board, so be sure to keep adding to it as you find new items that appeal to you.

# Evidence Journals

The third advanced technique for powering up your affirmations is the use of an evidence journal. An evidence journal is a log book of all the evidence you're going to find that proves your affirmations are starting to work for you.

Get yourself a notebook or a beautiful journal to write in and put your affirmation at the top of a new page. If you have several affirmations that you're working with, use a new page for each one.

Once you've decided on your affirmations and written them into your evidence journal, make it a point to look for proof that what you're trying to manifest is getting closer, or that it's on its way to you. For example, if you're trying to get a better paying job or to increase your income and you find a dime on the sidewalk, instead of dismissing it as random chance, pick it up, say a silent "thank you" to the Universe for increasing your income today, and be sure to log this event in your journal: "Found ten cents today!".

Focusing on small bits of evidence
that your affirmations are starting to work
sends the message to the Universe
that you are ready to accept
more into your life.

It may not be much, but it's ten cents more than you had yesterday and you didn't have to do anything to get it except pick it up. It's a gift from the Universe;

choose to see it as proof that increased abundance is already flowing to you. Likewise, if someone buys you a cup of coffee or if you get a free sample or if your local department store scratch-and-save promotion nets you 20% off, log these things into your evidence journal as signs that your abundance is starting to increase.

What this does is it gets you into the right alignment for 1) recognizing opportunities when they appear, 2) *accepting* blessings that come your way, and 3) being grateful for all that is yours.

This may seem simplistic but it's so important. When you are trying to manifest something into your life, you have to be aware enough to realize it when it shows up and you have to be willing to reach out and grab it when you see it. After all, who hasn't had the experience of lamenting a lost opportunity that you either didn't realize was there until it was gone, or that you didn't act fast enough to take advantage of while it was available?

By tuning into the little opportunities and bits of abundance that come into your life, you start to create a habit of accepting abundance – you make it clear to the Universe that you're *ready* to allow increasing abundance into your life. And that opens the gates to the bigger things you're really after.

# Chapter 7:
# Moving Forward

A POSITIVE ATTITUDE CAUSES A CHAIN REACTION
OF POSITIVE THOUGHTS, EVENTS AND OUTCOMES.
IT IS A CATALYST AND IT SPARKS
EXTRAORDINARY RESULTS.
~WADE BOGGS

Now that you have learned the ins-and-outs of effective affirmations you can start using them to create the kind of life you really want for yourself. You can start using them to bypass the sneaky negative thought patterns that have been keeping you stuck in place for so long and start moving forward towards a brighter future.

You know now that affirmations are a powerful technique to help you bypass your inner critic and reprogram the negative beliefs that you might not even be aware you had – beliefs that, up until now, have been sabotaging your best efforts to achieve your biggest dreams and goals.

This doesn't mean that you'll never be plagued by negative thoughts again, because you will be. That's just part of being human. You also grew up listening to other people's doubts, and over the years you internalized these negative patterns and made them your own. Realistically, you're not going to change that lifetime habit overnight. You will continue to encounter negativity throughout your life. But now you know what to do about it.

## Ready, Set, Go!

Now you have the ability to recognize your ingrained, automatic thought habits for what they are. You know the effect those negative thoughts have been having in your life, and you're ready to tackle them head-on!

**You're ready** to make a deliberate choice and a deliberate change for the positive.

**You're ready** to let go of what weighs you down and to step forward into a more positive, more hopeful, and more productive state of mind.

**You're ready** to start using the power of your own mind to build yourself up and create your dreams, rather than letting your own thoughts tear you apart.

**You're ready** to align yourself with your greatest potential, and the highest version of yourself that you are capable of becoming.

Your affirmations will help you with all of this. By making it a point to align yourself with the positive rather than sinking into despair and negativity, you start changing your default operating system.

Instead of accepting failure and misery as inevitable, you automatically begin to see potential new realities when things aren't going well. You find the paths and solutions that will allow you to *create* these better potential realities in your physical world. And you find within you the determination and self-confidence to see your actions through.

## Next Steps

By shifting your belief system and soaking your subconscious thought patterns in your new affirmations, you will make it much easier for the things and experiences you want to manifest into your life. My suggestion is that you:

- Review the Five-Step Process for creating affirmations that work in Chapter 3;

- Create two or three personal affirmations for the situation you're currently dealing with; and,
- Start using your new affirmations today!

If you run into problems coming up with specific affirmations, use the examples in Appendix A as a starting point (or just use them as-is if they feel right to you).

Remember that when you use your affirmations properly you are, in essence, changing your entire field of consciousness and allowing yourself to create a brand-new reality.

And that, my friend, makes real magic start to happen.

May your thoughts and your future be beautiful...

# Appendix:
# Example Affirmations

To help you get started creating your own affirmations, I'm including three sets of topic-specific affirmations for you to try out:

- Affirmations for stress relief
- Affirmations for motivation
- Affirmations for success

These sets are designed to help you out with three of the most common situations for which people first tend to try using affirmations.

To use these affirmations, my suggestion is that you write them out and read them over twice a day, first thing in the morning and last thing at night. If you'd like additional ideas on when to use your affirmations, be sure to refer to Chapter 4.

Also, please note that if any of these affirmations feel like too much of a stretch to you (if they don't feel believable), then try dialing them down a little. For example, if "I believe in myself and my goals" feels off, then modify it by saying "I am willing to believe in myself and my goals" or even "I am willing to believe that I could believe in myself and my goals."

When you've used your modified affirmations long enough that they no longer feel like any kind of a stretch, you know you've made an emotional shift (yay!), and you can dial them back up to stretch yourself a little bit further. Incremental changes, remember! Small progress is always better than no progress.

## Affirmations for Stress Relief

- My mind is becoming calm and clear.
- As my thoughts slow, my body relaxes.
- I am beginning to live a more balanced and peaceful life.
- My mind and body are relaxed and peaceful.
- My feelings of well-being are now increasing.
- Every day I become more peaceful and content.
- I am now in control of my life and my circumstances.
- I allow my mind and my body to become more and more relaxed.
- I know that having this time to myself is good for my health and well-being.
- I am enjoying this feeling of balance and peace.
- I feel calm and centred.
- I am naturally content and relaxed.

# Affirmations for Motivation

- I believe in myself and in my goals.
- I am learning to trust myself to achieve my goals.
- I am 100% committed to making my goals a reality.
- I have the power and ability to achieve my goals.
- I take action towards my goals every day.
- I am seeing consistent results from my actions.
- I am motivated and energized to achieve my goals.
- I am easily able to find any resources I require to achieve my goals.
- I enjoy taking action to make my goal a reality.
- I know that I will achieve my goal.

# Affirmations for Success

- Success comes naturally to me.
- I am successful in everything I choose to do.
- I am confident in my ability to succeed.
- Opportunities for success come to me constantly.
- I am easily able to handle anything that comes my way.
- I view challenges as opportunity for growth.
- Today has infinite possibilities!

- I am able to accomplish anything I set my mind to.
- I allow success to flow naturally into my life.
- I know that I will be successful!

# A Letter to the Reader

Dear Reader,

I hope you enjoyed *The Positive Affirmations Handbook*. Thank you so much for taking time out of your busy schedule to read it!

As you know, reviews are the lifeblood of any book – especially for us indie authors. Without them, our books quickly disappear from book store search algorithms and fade into obscurity. And that makes the books very, very sad.

If you'd like to help make this particular book very, very happy, it would be thrilled if you could leave it a review. You can do that right here:

(Just scan the QR code, and then click the "Write a Customer Review" button at the bottom of the page). Thanks so much, from both me and my book, and have a fantastic day!

Light and love,
Nathalie Thompson

# Other Books By This Author

*The Positive Affirmations Handbook*
*fearLESS*

## The Life Shifting Series:

*Mind Shifting*
*Soul Shifting*
*Body Shifting (Coming Soon!)*

## The Simple Strategies Series:

*Simple Strategies for Stress Relief*
*Simple Strategies for Mindfulness*

## Coloring Books:

*Mystical Mantras Coloring Book*
*Celtic Knots Coloring Book*

Want to be the first to know when new books are published?
Sign up for the author's newsletter at www.NathalieThompson.com!

# About the Author

**Nathalie Thompson** wants to live in a world where coffee pots are never empty and everyone is living the extraordinary life of their dreams.

A transformation catalyst and motivational expert, she is the author of *fearLESS* and *Mind Shifting* and her articles have been featured on the *Huffington Post* and on the blogs of NYT best-selling inspirational authors Pam Grout and Mike Dooley.

Connect with her and start transforming *your* dreams into reality over at www.VibeShifting.com!

/vibeshifting          @vibeshifting

# References

[1]http://www.merriam-webster.com/dictionary/mantra
[2] http://pss.sagepub.com/content/20/7/860
[3] https://faculty.washington.edu/chudler/words.html
[4] http://www.pinterest.com/vibeshifting